A LITTLE
BOOK OF
BIG DREAMS

A Little Book of Big Dreams

by Alan C. Elliott

Rutledge Hill Press®
Nashville, Tennessee
A Thomas Nelson Company

Published by Rutledge Hill Press®, a Thomas Nelson company, P.O. Box 141000, Nashville, Tennessee 37214.

ISBN 1-55853-897-6

Printed in Colombia
1 2 3 4 5 6 7 8 9—05 04 03 02 01

*For Annette,
Mary, and William,
who made me the
richest man in
the world.*

Preface

THE PURPOSE OF this book is to show you by example how ordinary Americans have accomplished extraordinary successes— in business, life, or in service to others.

You hold in your hands a packet of idea-seeds that will help you march forward in your life. If you take these messages to heart, they will change you from spectator to participant in the American Dream. These are entertaining, informative, and sometimes humorous stories about people just like you who became innovators, inventors, entertainers, business leaders, scientists, educators, dreamers, and overcomers.

Be warned. There are no magic pills that will make you a success overnight. You must take an active role in your own success. Andrew Carnegie's motto was "Anything in life worth having is worth working for!" If your goal is to have a successful marriage, you must work for it. If you want to become wealthy, you must work for it. If you want to be an entertainer or sports hero, you must work for it. If you want to serve humanity, you must work for it. Since you must work, make the most of it. Work smart as well as hard, run with enthusiasm, be patient, be persistent, and relish the journey.

May your dreams come true!

Acknowledgments

MANY PEOPLE HELPED me gather this information and put these stories together. Thanks to my researchers, Beverly Woodward and Angie Hoffman. Thanks to the many people or associates of the people mentioned in this book that took time to personally correspond or talk with me. Readers who plowed through the stories to help make them better and more readable include Patsy Summey, Betty Brooks, Evelyn Langston, Mary Spencer, Ron and Linda Cawthon, Wayne Woodward, and Lori Moores. Thanks to Nicholas Smith for his efforts in making this edition possible. Special thanks to my wife, Annette, for her encouragement, invaluable advice, and patience.

— ALAN C. ELLIOTT

A Little
Book of
Big Dreams

George Lucas

"I set out to make a film for a generation growing up without fairy tales."
—George Lucas

GROWING UP IN Modesto, California, George Lucas watched every adventure serial he could find. These short action films were stories of good versus evil, full of fights, chase scenes, and suspenseful cliff-hangers. When George needed inspiration for his own films, he returned in his mind to the films that excited him during his youth. Lucas graduated from the University of Southern California and, with his friend Francis Ford Coppola, formed a production company called American Zoetrope. His first feature, a science-fiction story called *THX-1138*, was the origin of the now famous THX "The audience is listening" advanced theater sound logo. In 1973, Lucas's film *American Graffiti* was successful enough to give boosts to the careers of Ron Howard and Richard Dreyfus.

His third film catapulted Lucas to instant fame. Working with a brilliant team of up-and-coming special-effects wizards, Lucas's new company, Industrial Light and Magic, created the dazzling effects for *Star Wars*. The sci-fi fairy tale, which merged cutting-edge effects with a strong story of good versus evil inspired by the early serials, took the world by storm. Lucas followed with *The Empire Strikes Back* and *Return of the Jedi*, and again used the serial formula successfully in the Indiana Jones trilogy. In 1992, with six mega-blockbusters under his belt, he received an Academy Award, the prestigious Irving G. Thalberg Life Achievement Award. Although he stumbled with a few of his later productions, Lucas continued to do his best work when he told stories using the technique that first inspired his love of film.

CONSIDER THIS: What makes you excited and passionate about your work? Use the energy you feel in your own life to get your message across to others.

Ray Kroc

"Common sense is instinct, and enough of it is genius."
—GEORGE BERNARD SHAW

RAY KROC WANTED to be a winner. For fifty-seven of his years he made a good living but never hit the jackpot. However, he kept his eyes open for an opportunity. As a salesman for a milk shake company, he was impressed by an order from a small hamburger stand in California that needed to make forty-eight shakes at a time. When he investigated, he found two brothers, Maurice and Richard McDonald, turning out hamburgers as quickly as they could be made. They had simplified the standard restaurant operation. As one of the brothers recalled: "Out went dishes, glasses, and silverware. Out went service, the dishwashers, and the long menu. We decided to serve just hamburgers, drinks, and french fries on paper plates. Everything prepared in advance, everything uniform."

Kroc wanted a taste of the McDonalds' success and hounded the brothers until they agreed to allow him to sell franchises. During the next six years, Kroc sold 200 McDonald franchises. In only twenty-two years, McDonald's became a billion-dollar company. The ingredients that led to the success of McDonald's over all others are simple. The menu is brief, containing only items whose consistent quality can be maintained in thousands of stores. There are strict standards for service, cleanliness, and store operations—and the standards are enforced. The company constantly researches its market (mostly families with children) to determine what customers want, and utilizes prolific and efficient advertising to carry its message to consumers.

CONSIDER THIS: The plan is simple: quality, consistency, cleanliness, and good value. Most people will agree with the plan, but only the winner will implement it with passion.

Edison's Bright Idea

"Genius is 1 percent inspiration and 99 percent perspiration."
—THOMAS EDISON

IN 1878, WHEN Thomas Edison announced that he would have a working small electric light "in a matter of weeks," gas stocks plummeted. Riding on his already legendary reputation, Edison raised money, organized the Edison Electric Light Company, and set out to invent the electric light. The trick was simply to find the correct element for the light filament. Thousands of materials were tested, but none lasted beyond a few seconds. After months of failure, Edison hired a physics expert named Francis Upton. With Upton's help, experimentation focused on a platinum filament, which showed some promise. It was now 1879. Work began early each morning, and Edison spent most of the day flitting from workbench to workbench observing the trials. At night he played songs at his pipe organ while he mulled over the day's findings in his mind. By mid-1879 it was clear that the platinum lamp would not work.

In October 1879, Upton and Edison's assistant Charles Bachelor began researching carbon. They devised a lamp with a short carbonized thread in a vacuum. Beginning on October 21, 1879, the carbonized lamp remained lit for forty hours. The process had been messy, discouraging, and very non-romantic, but success was finally achieved. Edison believed the electric light could be produced. He placed his reputation on the line and endured more than a thousand failures before seeing that first successful lamp.

CONSIDER THIS: If you have a good idea, work toward its completion. The road may be difficult and discouraging, but the success will be sweet.

Dave Thomas

"Don't just study people who succeed, study people who handle success well."

—DAVE THOMAS

DAVE THOMAS WAS adopted by a loving family, but his mother died when he was only five. His father remarried three times, and the family moved more than a dozen times before Dave reached his mid-teens. The only constant in his life was his grandmother, who gave him security and taught him the pleasure of hard work. Dave remembers first learning about restaurants because his father took him out to eat quite often. Since he liked to eat, Dave thought that owning a restaurant would be a great career. He took a job at a Hobby House restaurant, and when his father moved again, Dave stayed behind. At age fifteen, he was on his own.

During the Korean War, Dave joined the army and attended its Cook and Baker's School. After the war, he was given the opportunity to manage four Kentucky Fried Chicken restaurants. Dave learned the business well and in 1968 sold his KFC stock to begin his own chain of restaurants named after his daughter Wendy. His concept was to create a better hamburger—made from fresh meat, made to order, and served in a relaxed, family atmosphere. Wendy's grew rapidly until Thomas stepped out of the leadership in 1982. After several years of falling sales and declining quality, Thomas returned to the company as its "spokesman, in-house cheerleader, and roaming quality-control man." Once back under the founder's watchful eye, Wendy's rebounded and once again began to prosper.

CONSIDER THIS: Success is a long-term proposition. It requires constant attention to the guiding principles that made you successful to begin with.

Steinway Quality

> *"Music is the universal language of mankind."*
> —HENRY WADSWORTH LONGFELLOW

HEINRICH STEINWEG WAS born in the small German Hartz Mountain hamlet of Wolfshagen. Beginning in 1806, young Heinrich experienced a series of tragedies that wiped out most of his family. Orphaned, he joined the Prussian army and became a bugler. Despite having no formal training, Heinrich was an able musician, entertaining the troops on the zither and pianoforte. When he left the army, he became a church organist and began to build pianos in his kitchen at night. Although Heinrich worked in primitive facilities, people recognized the high quality of his work. But as his business prospered, revolution forced Heinrich and his family to move to America.

Settling in New York City, the family name was anglicized to Steinway. Heinrich and his three sons took jobs with different piano makers to learn the details of doing business in the United States. After three years of working for others, they started their own company, Steinway & Sons, producing one piano a week. The Steinway piano soon became known for its quality and clarity of sound. Steinway was more concerned with building the best rather than building the most, and Steinway pianos soon began to win awards. In 1872 Steinway Village, a Long Island mini-town that included employee housing, a school, library, and bathhouse, was opened. During tough economic times, companies offered Heinrich royalties to use the Steinway name on items such as radios. Since the Steinways could not control the quality of those products, they refused to compromise the integrity of their name. As a result, the Steinway name continues to be associated only with the finest musical instruments in the world.

CONSIDER THIS: A reputation built on quality must never be compromised.

Martin Luther King Jr.'s Dream

"I have a dream that one day . . . people will be judged more for the content of their character than the color of their skin."

—DR. MARTIN LUTHER KING JR.

AMERICANS LOVE TO dream about peace and prosperity. Some people dream only for themselves. Other people dream for us all. It is not surprising that a dreamer would come to the forefront of the civil rights movement in the 1960s. Dr. Martin Luther King Jr. was more than a gifted orator. His message of challenge and hope was fuller, more thought out, and more powerful than that of any other leader in the movement. He had a vision of the future in which all people would be given an equal chance for success and every person would be treated with dignity and respect. He painted a picture of the future based on his belief that God wanted all of His children to live together in peace and with honor for each other. However, not everyone appreciated his message.

Leaders are often loved deeply by some and hated intensely by others. As a result, leaders must pay a price for standing at the forefront of a cause. For his courage to stand against prejudice and hate, Dr. King was assassinated. Fortunately, dreams are more powerful than one person's life. Dreams based on truth, dignity, and righteousness somehow stand against those who would destroy them. As long as leaders have enough character to stand up against evil and to fight for honor, righteousness, and dignity, America will continue to grow closer to its dream of peace and prosperity for all of its citizens.

CONSIDER THIS: Open your eyes and determine where people are being treated unfairly. Be quick to respond. Use your influence to bring about equality and integrity among those with whom you deal.

Mae Jemison Is First in Space

"Hope is the thing with feathers that perches in the soul."
—EMILY DICKINSON

WHEN *STAR TREK* took to the small screen in the 1960s, it not only introduced concepts of space exploration, it crossed a barrier by involving minorities in major leadership roles on the starship *Enterprise*. For young Mae Jemison, the role of Lieutenant Uhura was particularly exciting. As an African-America girl interested in science and space, she found no role models in the all-white and all-male astronauts going into space. Yet, in the fictional world of *Star Trek,* she found a like mind. When Mae graduated from high school, she entered Stanford and received degrees in chemical engineering and African-American history. Following her undergraduate studies, she earned a medical degree from Cornell.

Mae's interests extend beyond the scientific. She served with the Peace Corps in Africa, has learned three foreign languages (Russian, Swahili, and Japanese), and is an accomplished amateur dancer. In 1985, Dr. Jemison interviewed at NASA and received encouragement from Robert McNair, one of the first African-American astronauts. Mae was accepted as an astronaut candidate in 1987 and in September 1992 became the first African-American woman in space. Each day she began her work shift quoting Lieutenant Uhura's words, "Hailing frequencies open!" Since her stint aboard the space shuttle, Dr. Jemison has often taken time from her busy work schedule to speak to children and encourage them to follow their dreams.

CONSIDER THIS: America is a land of many opportunities, but they are not given to you without cost. You often must struggle, study hard, and overcome substantial obstacles to realize your own American Dream.

Kresge's Change for the Better

"The old order changeth, yielding place to new."
—Alfred lord Tennyson

HARRY CUNNINGHAM WENT to work for the Kresge Company in 1928 as a stockroom trainee. Gradually, Harry was promoted to better jobs, and management noticed his good ideas. In 1957 he was appointed a vice president with an assignment to study the marketplace to determine the best plan for the company's future. Harry logged over 200,000 miles of travel and began to believe that discounting was the wave of the future. In 1959 Cunningham was made president of the Kresge Company but did not make the switch to discounting immediately. He instructed his executives to study the discount industry. Little by little, Kresge's management saw that discounting was holding a growing share of the retail market, and in March 1961 made the decision to move into discounting.

Forty KMart stores were opened by 1963, and the number swelled to more than a thousand stores by 1977. Hiring and training good management for those stores was difficult, and the company actively recruited at over 100 colleges and universities. Future management was trained in small discount stores named Jupiter. In 1976 KMart surpassed JCPenney as the nation's second-largest retailer. In a changing and competitive marketplace, KMart continues to find its share of success. It has responded to market challenges by emphasizing quality management, high-turnover merchandise, across-the-board discounting, and by clustering stores in a single market area to aid in advertising.

CONSIDER THIS: Organizations that refuse to adapt to the trends of society will vanish. Are you studying your competition to see how you will be able to adjust to the new order when it comes?

Wrigley Didn't Overlook the Little Things

> *"When business is good it pays to advertise; when business is bad you've got to advertise."*
> —Anonymous

BILL WRIGLEY WAS a problem child. He was thrown out of school and was always "up to no good." At the age of thirteen he was taken out of school and put to work stirring pots of boiling soap at his father's factory. His father later decided to try the boy as a salesman and sent him to the small towns of New England. Bill soon demonstrated that he could sell. He readily made friends on the road and made it a point "to be always polite, always patient, and never to argue." At the age of twenty, in 1891, Bill struck out on his own. He moved to Chicago and became a sales representative for a baking powder company. As an incentive to those buying his product, he included two sticks of chewing gum with every package. It was just a sales gimmick, but he kept getting requests for more gum. The requests increased to the point that Wrigley was selling more gum than powder, and he eventually dropped all other products and concentrated on promoting the gum.

By 1910, Wrigley's Spearmint was the top-selling gum in the country, and his Juicy Fruit gum was not far behind. In 1915 Wrigley sent free sticks of gum to 1.5 million telephone subscribers. Later he repeated the mail-out to 7 million people. Wrigley poured more marketing money into advertising his gum than any other single product advertiser of the day. Despite the fact that a pack of gum sold for only five cents, Wrigley amassed a fortune and used it to create a giant financial empire.

CONSIDER THIS: Look for clues about what you are doing now that could turn into big business if you gave it the chance.

The Band-Aid

"To accept good advice is but to increase one's own ability."
—JOHANN WOLFGANG VON GOETHE

EVEN WHEN HUNDREDS or thousands of people hear a good idea, it is the rare individual who does something about it. Robert Johnson was a co-owner of the Seabury & Johnson company when he attended a meeting during which Joseph Lister described the science of bacteriology and made a plea for sanitary conditions in hospitals. The year was 1876, and most of those in attendance listened with skepticism. It was hard to imagine those little "bugs" causing problems. However, Johnson was convinced that Lister was on to something, and he talked his brothers Edward and James into developing products that would help make hospitals more sanitary.

In 1886 the brothers formed their own company, Johnson & Johnson, and began promoting their sterilized gauze. By 1910 the company needed forty buildings to produce a growing line of medical products. One day Earle E. Dickson, a cotton buyer in the company's purchasing department, showed a co-worker a self-stick bandage he had developed and was using at home. Earle had put a dab of sterile cotton and gauze on a strip of surgical tape to create a bandage that he could use to take care of his family's cuts and scrapes. He placed a crinoline fabric on the sticky parts of the bandage until it was needed. James Johnson saw one of the bandages and immediately recognized its potential in the marketplace. The invention was dubbed the "Band-Aid," and it soon became one of the world's most recognized trademarks.

CONSIDER THIS: Listen to the ideas of those around you. New ideas are often the basis of new products and perhaps new companies.

Peter Jennings

"If a man bites a dog, this is news."
—John Bogart

ALTHOUGH PETER JENNINGS' father (who was a distinguished broadcast journalist for the Canadian Broadcasting Corporation) may have helped him get his first broadcasting job, Peter still had to prove that he could be a first-class journalist. His early chance came at CBC, where he hosted a half-hour radio show for children. Peter showed promise and dedication, and was soon allowed to host several public affairs programs. Eventually, he became a special events commentator and the host of Vue, a late-night talk show. In 1964 Peter's coverage of the Democratic National Convention in Atlantic City impressed ABC News President Elmer Lower. Lower immediately offered Peter a job as an ABC correspondent, but he turned it down. Three months later, Peter woke up in a cold sweat one night and thought, "What have I done?" He wrote Lower back and got the job.

In 1965, in an effort to boost their national broadcast ratings, ABC made Jennings the anchor of their nightly newscast. Although he did a good job, he did not have the qualifications to compete with Cronkite and Huntley and Brinkley. Jennings returned to reporting in 1968 and established himself as one of the foremost foreign correspondents. His in-depth analysis of the news gained him award after award. In 1983 Jennings was named sole anchor for the ABC *Nightly News*. As he looks back on his career, Jennings admits that it was the role model of his father that pushed him to continue, to strive to be the best. "I'm still trying to live up to my father's standards."

CONSIDER THIS: Pick a mentor with the kinds of attributes you desire. An example of excellence can give you the motivation to do and become your best.

Face Your Troubles Squarely

"Three things give hardy strength: sleeping on hairy mattresses, breathing cold air, and eating dry food."
—WELSH PROVERB

THEODORE ROOSEVELT WAS a weakling. Does that surprise you? As a child, Roosevelt was thin, in poor health, timid, and afraid of getting hurt. The Roosevelt family took trips to find places more amenable to young "Teddy's" ailments. When he became a teenager, Teddy decided to conquer his frailty. After traveling to parts of America and Europe, it was apparent that a simple change of climate would not cure the adolescent's health problems. Teddy decided to immerse himself in physical activity.

His formula was to do things he was afraid of doing, so he became a cowboy in the Dakotas. In that campaign to improve his strength and courage, Teddy at one time or another broke his wrist, his arm, his nose, his ribs, and his shoulder. After entering Harvard, he took up boxing. Although Teddy was often "beat to a pulp," he became an adequate fighter and even fought in a championship match (he lost). In the Spanish-American War, Teddy was a lieutenant colonel in the "Rough Riders," where he became a hero for his exploits at the battle of San Juan Hill. It was because of his "Rough Rider" image that Roosevelt became a popular military and political figure, and was elected governor of New York in 1898. He was elected vice president of the United States in 1900, and after President McKinley died in 1901, Roosevelt became president.

CONSIDER THIS: Struggle often provides us with our most productive times of growth. The caterpillar gains strength in its struggle to tear out of its cocoon. Without the struggle, it does not have the strength to fly. Can we step back while we are in the midst of a struggle and see how it will give us strength and insight for the future?

Tom Landry Learns Football

> *"Coaching: To get people to do what they don't want to do in order to achieve what they want to achieve."*
>
> —TOM LANDRY

IN THE SMALL town of Mission, Texas, during the Great Depression, a scrappy boy by the name of Tommy Landry began learning about the game of football. There were no organized leagues for kids, so Tommy and his friends would stage their own games on a field near his house. They played thousands of football games, often stopping only when their moms demanded that they come home for supper. Tommy played center and quarterback, coached, and organized the games. But he needed more than a small-town sandlot league to set him on the track to becoming one of America's greatest sports legends. He needed a coach.

When young Tom entered Mission High School, he was fortunate to become a member of Bill Martin's junior-varsity team. Tom thrived on the competition provided by football. The fanaticism of Friday night football in Texas, combined with the increasing success of the Mission team under Coach Martin, ignited a blaze of enthusiasm throughout the entire community. During Mission's 1941 championship season, Tom experienced his most memorable and sweetest victories. After World War II, Tom became a gridiron star at the University of Texas, then went on to play and coach in the National Football League. His astoundingly successful reign as coach of the Dallas Cowboys from 1960 through 1988, which led to his enshrinement in the Pro Football Hall of Fame, possibly never would have occurred had it not been for the experience he gained under Coach Martin as a youngster in Mission, Texas.

CONSIDER THIS: Raw talent plus effective coaching equals success. Seek and hire the most talented people possible, then train them to be their best.

Jay Leno's Big Break

**"Laffing is the sensation ov Pheeling good all over,
and showing it principally in one spot."**
—JOSH BILLING

JAY LENO WAS headed for a career of flipping burgers. He brought home poor grades and was known as the class clown. Even when slicing potatoes into fries at a McDonald's, he earned a reputation as a "cut-up." Jay remembers hating homework until his English teacher, Mrs. Hawkes, encouraged him to write down some of his funny stories as a creative writing assignment. Suddenly, Jay was spending hours writing and rewriting his stories. When he read them in class, he got laughs, and that encouraged him to create more funny stories.

Jay spent plenty of time in detention. Luckily, the overseeing teacher, Mr. Walsh, liked his stories. One day he asked Jay, "Why don't you go into show business?" That was a new concept for Jay—and it was the beginning of a dream. He got his first break as the French Fry Cut-Up in a McDonald's talent show and won $150. While in college, Jay began learning the comedy craft by performing in non-paying, low-paying, and often sleazy joints. After spending years in New England, he decided to try his luck in California. Jay played comedy clubs and began to land small roles on TV sitcoms and in movies. To a comedian, a successful appearance on *The Tonight Show* is the ultimate break. It eluded Jay until one night when Steve Martin dropped by the club where he was performing. Martin liked what he saw and talked to the people at *The Tonight Show*, and Jay got his chance on March 2, 1977. His first *Tonight Show* performance drew big laughs and a "wink" from Johnny Carson, and Jay was on his way to stardom.

CONSIDER THIS: Big breaks come to those whose hard work and talents prepare them for their "moment of judgment."

Colonel Sanders

> *"Genius, that power which dazzles humans,*
> *is oft but perseverance in disguise."*
> —H. W. AUSTIN

BEFORE BEGINNING HIS famous franchise, Col. Harland Sanders worked as a streetcar conductor, a railroad fireman, a justice of the peace, an insurance salesman, and held other occupations. In 1930, at the age of forty, he was operating a service station in Corbin, Kentucky, when he decided to offer food to his customers. At first, he served them right off the dining table in his living quarters. His food was popular, and he eventually opened a restaurant across the street from the station. Over a period of years, Sanders developed the secret combination of eleven herbs and spices that went into his chicken recipe. But when a new interstate highway bypassed his town, Sanders sold his business and began collecting Social Security. That could have been the end of the story, but the colonel decided that he was not ready for the retired life.

At the age of sixty-six, Sanders took to the road in an old station wagon. Every time he saw a restaurant, he stopped, knocked on the door, and prepared a batch of his special recipe chicken. Restaurant owners made handshake deals to use the recipe and pay Sanders a nickel for every chicken they sold. After the Kentucky Fried Chicken recipe was introduced, most of the restaurants found that their customers couldn't get enough of the "finger lickin' good" chicken. Success blossomed and KFC restaurants were franchised throughout the United States and around the globe. In a poll taken in the late 1970s, Colonel Sanders was listed as one of the five most recognized persons in the entire world.

CONSIDER THIS: It's never too late to begin, but once you begin, it often takes enthusiasm, perseverance, and patience to realize success.

Earl Tupper's Party Plan

*"The most successful men have used seeming failures
as stepping-stones to better things."*
—GRENVILLE KLEISER

WHILE HE WAS still in his teens, Earl Tupper began a small business selling fruits and vegetables to his neighbors. He was good at it and learned quickly about the finer points of salesmanship. This was a big asset to Tupper when, years later, he began a new business. That enterprise, started in 1945, was a line of plastic containers that he dubbed Tupperware. At first, Tupper used the conventional method of marketing his products through retail stores. But after five years of mediocre sales, he began to envision a new plan of action. Recalling his earlier days, when he sold produce directly to housewives, Tupper decided to try this same direct approach in selling Tupperware.

It was 1950 when Tupper began selling his plastic containers directly to the people who would use them most. He invited people into homes and demonstrated the product. Sales were good, better than they had been in retail stores, and it was clear that this approach had considerable promise. However, it was also clear that Tupper could not sell enough product by himself, so he arranged for housewives to become Tupperware dealers. They could hold "parties" at friends' houses, and each hostess would receive a gift. The housewives would have a part-time income, while maintaining the freedom to take their children to school and do the other household chores. By 1954, Tupperware had a network of over 9,000 dealers across the United States. Sales eventually spread to Europe, and today Tupperware is found in kitchen cabinets around the world.

CONSIDER THIS: A product alone is not enough. You must devise a plan to sell your product, sometimes with a unique method, to your customers.

Bill Gates

"Only the paranoid survive."
—Intel CEO Andrew Grove

BILL GATES IS the Edison and Ford for our times. He became a success not just by being in the right place at the right time, but by being prepared, intelligent, committed, and lucky. As a young student he and Paul Allen, his future partner, began playing around with computers on a clunky teletype terminal and got jobs finding bugs in computer programs. Bill helped write a scheduling program for his school and included instructions that put him into classes with the girls of his choice.

While attending Harvard, Bill became even more committed to computing and saw a technical revolution coming. He and Allen created a BASIC language interpreter for the first wave of microcomputers. However, Bill's company was just one among thousands fighting for a share of the microcomputer market. He hired the brightest minds he could find, and his Microsoft firm competed well and established itself as a "language" company. Microsoft's big break came when IBM was searching for a company to help it write an operating system for the new IBM personal computer. IBM initially went to another company that was already marketing the leading micro-operating system, called C/PM. The other company was reluctant to sign IBM's non-disclosure agreement, so the company continued its search. When IBM approached Microsoft, Bill saw the potential and grabbed the deal. The resulting PC-DOS and MS-DOS operating systems established Microsoft's dominance in the software market and were the foundations for Windows and many other popular application programs.

CONSIDER THIS: If you want to be lucky, be smart and be prepared. Hire the brightest people you can afford, and fight to take advantage of every opportunity.

Anne Sullivan and Helen Keller

*"We can do anything we want to do if
we stick with it long enough."*

—HELEN KELLER

WHEN HELEN KELLER suffered an illness that made her blind and deaf, she gradually adopted animal instincts in order to survive. That is how teacher Anne Sullivan found Helen when she arrived in Tuscumbia, Alabama, to teach the child. What transpired next was a clear example of tough love, leadership, and discipline. Sullivan literally had to fight Helen and attempted to communicate with her through the sensation of touch, the only real sense the youngster still recognized. Week after week, Anne pressed her hand into Helen's, making symbols with the positions of her fingers against Helen's palm. She was spelling out words, but to Helen, it made no sense. When Helen finally understood the relationship between the word "water" and the patterns pressed on her palm, Helen remembered, "I was caught up in the first joy I had known since my illness."

Anne was tough on her pupil. "As soon as I knew right from wrong," Helen wrote, "she put me to bed whenever I committed a misdeed." The story of Anne and Helen has become an American wonder, as the physically challenged girl eventually grew up to be one of the brightest minds of her time. Helen became a communicator and a symbol of the power that people have to rise above difficult circumstances, but she did not (could not) do it on her own. Anne Sullivan demanded that her pupil learn beyond all expectations and gave her love and fulfillment in return.

CONSIDER THIS: Whom are you teaching and encouraging? How are you making them stretch beyond their expectations? What persons are waiting for you to encourage them into discovering their own genius?

Wal-Mart Buys American

"There are efforts and there are results. And it is the strength of the effort that usually determines the size of the result."
—E. F. GIRARD

SAM WALTON BEGAN his retail career as a management trainee for JCPenney. After a tour in the army, he opened a Ben Franklin store. Along with his brother, Sam opened more Ben Franklins until 1962, when he ventured into discount merchandising with his first Wal-Mart store. Sam focused mostly on small towns, and under his powerful leadership, the number of Wal-Mart stores grew quickly. Part of Wal-Mart's image and appeal has been its American character. It is a hometown place, with friendly people and a clean image. In 1985 Sam embarked on an ambitious campaign to buck the trend of buying imported merchandise and to institute a program that would encourage American manufacturers to produce more competitive goods.

To encourage domestic manufacturers, Wal-Mart provided long-term commitments and guaranteed orders to American firms. Calling the rising importation of goods a "threat to our free enterprise system," Wal-Mart's program provided several small companies with orders that allowed them to expand their operations and hire more workers. One shirt manufacturer moved some of its operations from offshore back to the United States to participate in Wal-Mart's program. The campaign not only provided Wal-Mart with quality merchandise, it resulted in a host of positive articles about the retailer in newspapers all over the country.

CONSIDER THIS: Imports will always be with us. The answer to preserving the American system of free enterprise is to meet the challenges with innovation, intelligence, and hard work.

Fritos Corn Chips

"The only way to get anywhere is to start from where you are."
—WILLIAM LEE

CHARLES DOOLIN OWNED an ice cream business in San Antonio, Texas, but during the depression, a price war erupted and he was unable to make a profit. Doolin looked around for other products to make and discarded countless ideas as unfeasible. One idea he discarded was the possibility of making some new product out of the Mexican tortilla, because they went stale too quickly. Doolin also took notice of the popular potato chip snack, but dismissed that idea since he wanted something unique. Then, one day while buying lunch, he saw and purchased a bag of a new corn chips snack called Fritos.

Doolin liked the new snack and tracked down the manufacturer—a native Mexican who offered to sell his entire operation for

$100 so he could move back to Mexico. Doolin couldn't afford the price and had to borrow part of the money from his mother. She helped him set up the production machinery in her own kitchen and, using a crude, converted potato ricer. They were soon turning out ten pounds of Fritos an hour. As word of the product spread, sales rose to as much as $10 per day. To meet the demand, Doolin developed a new, more efficient method of production. Eager to expand his successful operation, Doolin went on numerous sales trips. On some of those trips, he took a temporary job as a cook in the cities he was visiting, since he couldn't afford to pay himself a salary. The company grew slowly at first and then faster after the end of World War II. By the 1950s, Fritos was a household name and one of the nation's most popular snack foods.

CONSIDER THIS: Consider carefully what you might add as a new product. Discard those that aren't sufficiently promising, and dedicate yourself fully when you find a potential star.

Steven Spielberg

> *"To him that is determined it remains only to act."*
> —ITALIAN PROVERB

WHAT AND HOW we think has a lot to do with how much we can accomplish. If we believe we will succeed, our chances of success are great. If we cannot see ourselves as being successful, we will likely never experience our dreams. William James was a noted American psychologist. He wanted to discover the human factors that gave certain people the ability to succeed. One of the principles that James uncovered was the "As if" technique. Using "As if" means to act as if that which you desire is already in hand.

By the time he was thirteen years old, Steven Spielberg knew he wanted to be a movie director. When he was seventeen, he visited Universal Studios as a tourist. It was too much for him. He sneaked away from the tour and into the sound stage where a real movie was being made. Finding the head of the editorial department, young Steven talked to him about making films. The next day, Steven put on a suit, borrowed his father's briefcase, and walked onto the studio lot as if he belonged. He found an abandoned trailer and painted "Steven Spielberg, Director" on the door. He spent his summer "working" on the lot and learning everything he could about the movie-making business. In time, Spielberg became a studio regular, produced a short film, and was eventually offered a seven-year contract. Today, he is one of the world's most renowned film directors.

CONSIDER THIS: Know what you want to be. Dream your goals. Learn everything you can about what you want to become. Associate with those who can take you where you want to go. Step out with confidence and begin working.

American by Choice

"Be honest, work hard, and don't be afraid to take a chance."
—SAM ZIADY'S FATHER

AMERICA HAS LONG benefited from the energy and ideas brought by immigrant dreamers with pioneering spirits and can-do attitudes. One such dreamer was Sam Ziady from Beirut, Lebanon. In 1950, when he was nineteen, Sam's father gave him enough money to begin studies at South Carolina's Columbia Bible College. To continue his studies, Sam sold Bibles and dictionaries door-to-door during the summer. As he worked his way though college and then a master's program at the University of South Carolina, he expanded his business by hiring other students. When Chase Manhattan offered Sam an executive position, he was on the verge of realizing his dream of a banking career.

"Why do you want to work for Chase Manhattan Bank for $7,200?" asked his father when Sam returned to Beirut for a visit. "Security," said Sam. "How much did you make last summer with your door-to-door business?" asked his father. "Seventeen thousand dollars," said Sam. "Why do you need security? You have a master's degree, you are young, and you speak three languages," said his father, who encouraged Sam to expand his success in book selling. Sam took his father's advice, returned to America, and started the National Book Company. When he became a U.S. citizen, he changed his name to Sam Moore. His book business grew, and in 1968 Sam bought the American division of Thomas Nelson Publishers, one of the world's oldest publishing companies. His biography is called *American by Choice* because, he says, "Only in America would a Lebanese immigrant have the opportunity to become one of the nation's leading publishers."

CONSIDER THIS: You are what you are by choice. To achieve success, you must choose your dreams carefully and work smart and hard to bring them to fruition.

Clarence Birdseye

"Take time to deliberate, but when the time for action arrives, stop thinking and go in."

—ANDREW JACKSON

CLARENCE BIRDSEYE WAS sure he would make something of himself. He was the son of a New York Supreme Court judge and the grandson of a successful inventor. However, by the age of forty, Clarence had not yet managed to find a successful career. In 1923 he began evaluating his talents and knowledge in the hope of discovering something he could do well. The idea he settled on was inspired by a practice he had seen some ten years earlier in Labrador. The Eskimos there placed their freshly caught fish on the sub-zero snow and froze them instantly. Months later, when the fish were cooked, they still tasted fresh.

Birdseye did some extensive research and discovered that the reason the Eskimos' fish tasted fresh after lengthy storage was that they had been frozen so quickly. He consulted nutritionists and was told, "You've got a great idea." Birdseye worked on a technique to freeze fish quickly and by 1924 had perfected a device called a "belt froster." He received preliminary financial backing and built a freezer forty feet long. The enterprise he formed became known as General Foods Company. Although the quick-freezing idea had considerable merit and made sense for long-term food storage, Clarence Birdseye spent many years experimenting with various marketing approaches before frozen foods became commonplace in grocery stores.

CONSIDER THIS: Have you ever stopped to think what ideas you have had in the past may be worth a second look?

Oprah Winfrey

"I have been driven many times to my knees by the overwhelming conviction that I had nowhere else to go."
—ABRAHAM LINCOLN

OPRAH WINFREY'S EXPERIENCES as a child may account for her compassion for those in need and for her sensitive understanding of life's struggles. Born in a small Mississippi town in 1954, Oprah found little stability in her early homelife. She moved back and forth between separated parents and her grandmother, and eventually rebelled against life. However, even in the midst of uncertainty, Oprah found strength in faith, education, and the performing arts. While still in high school, she was hired by a local radio station to read the news. As a sophomore at Tennessee State University, she was picked as a reporter for a local television station. From there, Oprah became co-anchor of a news program in Baltimore and in 1984 was given a chance to revive a dying half-hour talk show called *A.M. Chicago*. Her emotional and honest style soon made the show a hit, and when its ratings surpassed the popular *Donahue Show*, it was renamed *The Oprah Winfrey Show* and expanded to one hour.

In 1985 Oprah appeared in the film *The Color Purple*, was nominated for an Academy Award, and was well on her way to stardom. Even with all her success, she remembers her spiritual roots. Her grandmother taught Oprah the importance of Bible study and prayer, and those lessons continue to be important in her life today. True to the message of the Bible, Oprah Winfrey shares her wealth with others, speaks up for those who are down-trodden, and challenges those who continue to live in bigotry.

CONSIDER THIS: Even when your beginnings are rough, you will do well to look forward to the future and to leave the troubles of the past behind.

Bette Nesmith's Liquid Paper

"Adopt the pace of nature; her secret is patience."
—RALPH WALDO EMERSON

BETTE NESMITH, LIKE many other secretaries in 1951, had a problem. When she made a mistake at the typewriter, it was difficult to erase. She had been a freelance artist, and it occurred to her that artists never erase, they simply paint over any mistakes. With that in mind, Bette tested a variety of concoctions in her kitchen until she devised a paint-like substance that she initially called "Mistake Out." Bette convinced the secretaries around her to begin using it, and an office supply dealer encouraged her to manufacture the paint. She was willing to do so and tried to find partners or someone else to provide financing, but everyone turned the idea down. Finally, Bette decided she would have to produce the paint on her own.

At first, she hired a college student to help sell the product, but the first year's sales amounted to only $1,142.71 and Bette's expenses were $1,217.35. As a single parent, Bette found it hard to juggle her new enterprise and a full-time secretarial position, so she took a part-time job in order to spend more time promoting her paint. She hired a chemist to develop a faster-drying formula and soon took the improved product on the road, demonstrating it to office supply dealers throughout the United States. After giving her sales presentation, Bette would leave behind twelve sample bottles. Eventually, her hard work paid off, and orders began to increase. The Liquid Paper Corporation continued to grow and was sold in 1979 for $47.5 million.

CONSIDER THIS: Even if an idea is good, it still may take the evangelism of a fanatic and the patience of Job before it will finally catch on.

Truett Cathy Is Closed on Sunday

"And on the seventh day God ended his work which he had made; and he rested on the seventh day."

—GENESIS 2:2

WHEN TRUETT CATHY left military service, he started the Dwarf House restaurant in Atlanta, Georgia. Since he lived next door to his restaurant, Truett worked virtually all day, every day—but he did not open on Sunday. Having become a Christian at the age of twelve, Truett felt that he could not be robbed of his day of rest. "If it takes seven days to make a living," he often said, "I ought to be doing something else."

The Dwarf House was successful, and Truett enjoyed experimenting with new dishes to serve his patrons. Some were well received, and some were not; however, there was one new idea that stood out above all the rest. It was called the Chick-fil-A, a specially prepared breast of chicken sandwich. Since it was so popular, Truett decided to try his sandwich in a fast-food location at a local mall. He opened his first Chick-fil-A store in Atlanta, and it was every bit as successful as he had hoped it would be. By the 1990s there were over 750 Chick-fil-A restaurants in the U.S., all still observing Truett's original "closed on Sunday" rule and many making better profits than seven-day restaurants next door. The Chick-Fil-A business is based on two principles: Glorify God in financial soundness, and have a positive influence on employees and customers. Teenage employees of Chick-fil-A stores are given college scholarships, and many have been given the opportunity to own their own business.

CONSIDER THIS: Stick to your principles, even if they go counter to popular wisdom.

The Beginnings of EDS

"The mass of men lead lives of quiet desperation."
— HENRY DAVID THOREAU

H. ROSS PEROT was sitting in a barbershop reading *Reader's Digest* when he saw this quote from Thoreau at the bottom of a page: "The mass of men lead lives of quiet desperation." Perot thought, "That's me. There I am." He was a good salesman for IBM, but felt he was not meeting his potential. As a salesman, Perot noticed that people were buying computers but really didn't know what to do with them. He had the idea of selling companies not only the computers, but also the software and staff to run them—an entire data processing department. IBM listened to Perot's idea but said that eighty cents of the computer dollar (at the time) was spent on hardware and only twenty cents on software. The twenty cents looked good to Perot, but IBM turned down his idea.

After the episode at the barbershop, Perot made the decision of his life. He quit IBM and spent $1,000 to start Electronic Data Systems (EDS). He had no computer and no staff, "just" an idea. At first, Perot bought time on an IBM 7070 mainframe computer and traveled throughout the country trying to sell that computing time. He visited seventy-nine companies before making his first sale. Since he had no staff, Perot had to find IBM 7070 operators who would help him during their off-time. Those individuals have never worked another day for Perot, but they continued on the payroll and received EDS stock when it was issued. According to Perot, "If those guys hadn't done the job for me, there would be no EDS."

CONSIDER THIS: There is that one moment in our lives when we decide to break out of a rut and move on to something greater. Is that moment right now for you?

Pepperidge Farm

*"An enterprise when fairly once begun, should not be
left till all that ought is won."*
—WILLIAM SHAKESPEARE

HOW MANY PEOPLE have become successful doing something
other than what they set out to do? Margaret Rudkin had never
baked a loaf of bread in her life. But her young son had asthma, and
the doctor suggested that, as part of her son's treatment, she bake
whole wheat bread from only natural ingredients. As her son
remembers, the first loaf came out like a brick, but gradually, as
Margaret experimented with the recipe, the bread became quite
tasty. It was soon the only bread served at the Rudkin house, and
visitors often would ask where they could purchase it. To see how
marketable her bread really was, Margaret baked twelve loaves, took

them to the local grocer, and had him taste it. The grocer immediately ordered more of the bread, and Margaret was in business.

The bread was first baked in the family kitchen, but as its popularity grew, the enterprise was moved to the family barns, which had been converted into kitchens. Margaret Rudkin was very particular about her product. If a loaf had not been wrapped neatly or if anything about the bread looked wrong, she would not let it be sold. Pepperidge Farm became well known for its tasty, high-quality products that consumers perceived to be a cut above other baked goods. Today, the company's products, including fresh baked products, biscuits, and frozen foods, are sold nationwide.

CONSIDER THIS: Even someone who has never tried his or her hand at a task can become a master, with patience and practice.

Michael Jordan

"If you work hard, you will get the things you want."
—JAMES JORDAN

AS A YOUNGSTER, Michael Jordan took sports seriously. He always wanted to win and he hated to lose. Standing only five feet ten inches tall, he made his high school's junior-varsity basketball team as a sophomore but was passed over in favor of another athlete when the coach needed a taller player for a state championship tournament. Michael never forgot that moment.

When he returned to school the next fall, Michael startled everyone, for over the course of the summer, he had grown five inches. "It was almost as if Michael willed himself taller," said his father. In order to gain more practice time, Michael began skipping classes. He eventually was suspended from school, and his father had to help the youngster strike a balance between academics and his commitment to sports. Michael took his father's advice but never lost any of his passion for winning. He continued to work harder than any of his teammates, and he also demanded more of himself. During his final season at the University of North Carolina, Michael was selected as college basketball's 1984 Player of the Year. Drafted that spring by the Chicago Bulls of the National Basketball Association, Michael Jordan became an instant sensation with his easygoing smile and slashing style of play. His formidable skills and dogged determination helped lift his new team from mediocrity to become one of the league's most successful franchises of all time.

CONSIDER THIS: If you know your talents and develop them passionately, you will earn success.

Cracker Barrel

*"There never was a day that couldn't be improved
by some good country cookin'."*
—CRACKER BARREL MENU

DAN EVINS OPERATED a small filling station business in
Tennessee during the 1960s, about the time the interstate highway
system was beginning to open up many rural areas. Wondering
how he could take advantage of the traffic, Dan realized that travelers would be hungry as well as in need of gasoline, so he considered selling food at his stations. At first, he thought about adding
fast food, which seemed to be the trend, but ultimately determined
that many people would rather have "real food" instead.

Dan decided to create a highway restaurant that would buck
the trend. He wanted his restaurant to be comfortable and reflect

the nostalgia of rural America. It would be like a country store, with big jars of candies and homemade jellies, potbellied stoves, handmade quilts and other quality items. With the help of some investor friends, Dan opened the original Cracker Barrel Old Country Store in 1969 as a family restaurant, gift shop, and service station. Travelers liked the idea, and soon people were standing in line to eat his country cooking. Dan obtained more investors and built more stores, eventually omitting the service station. By the late 1990s, over 300 Cracker Barrels had been opened. Dan believes that authentic country cooking, American values, and an honest-to-goodness rural lifestyle can be preserved, and he intends to do his part in his stores.

CONSIDER THIS: When everyone is following one trend, perhaps there is another important part of the market that is being forgotten. Someone will find it and service it. Will it be you?

KitchenAid

"If nobody else is going to invent a dishwasher, I'll do it myself."
—JOSEPHINE GARIS COCHRAINE

THE AUTOMATIC DISHWASHER took a long time to reach American homes after its invention in 1886. It all started when Josephine Garis Cochraine, the wife of an Illinois political leader, got mad at the servants who kept breaking her china. After one particularly bad evening, Josephine exploded at the kitchen staff and declared that she would invent a dishwasher, even though she had no mechanical experience and rarely washed dishes herself. Working in the woodshed, Josephine devised a contraption she dubbed the Garis-Cochraine, which proved to be such a good design that it was patented and won an award at the 1893 Columbian Exposition. Friends and business associates helped her establish a company, and the dishwashers it produced were sold to hotels and restaurants. Josephine directed the firm until her death in 1913.

In 1926 another company came into the picture. The Hobart company, founded in 1897, produced equipment for grocers and institutional kitchens. Hobart acquired the Garis-Cochraine but continued to concentrate on its heavy-duty dishwashers. It was not until 1949 that the company finally introduced a home model, called the KitchenAid. In its marketing research, Hobart found that many women of the period actually enjoyed washing dishes, so the company had to find a more compelling reason for women to buy the machine. Researchers also discovered that women felt guilty about leaving dirty dishes after late night snacks. That information, plus the added benefit of sterilization, led to dishwashers becoming a permanent fixture in many American homes.

CONSIDER THIS: A good idea may come before everyone is ready to use it. Timing must also be right.

Post-It Notes

"Self-trust is the essence of heroism."
—RALPH WALDO EMERSON

ART FRY, A scientist at 3M, was singing in the choir of North Presbyterian Church in St. Paul, Minnesota, and trying to mark his place in the hymnal with small pieces of paper. However, when he opened the book, the slips would invariably fall out. "What if there where a little adhesive on the paper to keep it in place?" Art thought to himself. He remembered a novel adhesive that had been invented some years earlier by another 3M scientist, Dr. Spencer Silver, and for over a year, Art conducted experiments to bring his adhesive bookmark to fruition. The work was not officially sanctioned, but 3M's corporate culture allows people to spend some of their time developing new ideas.

The right formula for the adhesive was difficult to determine. It had to be strong enough to hold the paper in place, but not so strong that it damaged the surface to which it adhered. Instead of using the pieces of paper as bookmarks, Art began to write notes on them and then stick them on things. He called the invention Post-It Notes. Sensing success, Art began to pass the notes out at meetings and finally got people at 3M to take notice, although there were still those who failed to see the value of the product. The company's first attempt at selling Post-It Notes was a disaster, but when the marketing department finally began passing out samples, the product took off like wildfire. Today, Post-It Notes are considered to be possibly the most important invention at 3M since Scotch brand transparent tape.

CONSIDER THIS: It often takes a champion, someone who really believes in a product, to push it past the corporate doubters to success in the marketplace. Does your organization encourage such champions?

Buster Brown

"Never forget a customer, never let a customer forget you."
—UNKNOWN

IF YOU DON'T know the Buster Brown Shoes character, you must have been living somewhere other than the United States. It is one of the most widely known symbols in American marketing. Buster Brown is also one of the first characters ever used to promote a product. The Brown Shoe Company was founded in 1878 and produced a line of shoes for boys and girls. In 1902 cartoonist Richard Outcault introduced a comic strip based on Buster Brown, his sister Mary Jane, and their dog Tige. John Bush, a sales executive for the Brown Shoe Company, recognized the sales potential that a tie-in with the cartoon character would create, and he soon purchased the rights to use Buster Brown to promote

Brown Shoes. The problem was that the Brown Shoe Company did not buy exclusive rights to the character, and the firm's owners were taken aback when the Buster Brown character was also used to promote whiskey and tobacco.

Bush was determined to make Brown Shoes' image of Buster Brown stick and hired a series of midgets to tour the country in costume. Ed Ansley devoted twenty-eight years to performing in a Buster Brown outfit and wore out five dogs in the process. With the advent of radio and television, Ed McConnell became Buster Brown. Today, surveys show that the Buster Brown logo is still widely recognized. In fact, many of the customers who bought their own pair of Buster Brown Shoes in the forties and fifties are now buying the same brand of footwear for their children.

CONSIDER THIS: The recognition of a logo can have long-term benefits and can even last from generation to generation.

Rose Blumkin's Superstore

> *"Probably the world's greatest humorist was the
> man who named them easy payments."*
> —STANISLAS

EVEN AT AGE ninety, Rose Blumkin could "run rings around" the top graduates of America's business schools and the Fortune 500 CEOs, stated a 1984 article in the *Wall Street Journal*. Rose emigrated from Russia to the United States in 1917, bribing her way past a border guard and traveling through China and Japan. The daughter of a poor rabbi, her success was due to a combination of brains, wit, and the determination to make something of herself. She told *Journal* reporter Frank James in 1984, "I'm born, thank God, with brains. In Russia you don't have no adding machine or nothing, so you have to use your head. So I always used it."

Rose Blumkin began her business career in a pawnshop at the age of forty-three. She ran the shop with her husband until his death 1950, and at that point she took off on her own. She established the Nebraska Furniture Mart, which became one of the largest furniture retailers in the U.S. However, things did not always go smoothly. During the Korean War, Blumkin had to borrow $50,000 on a short-term note to pay suppliers. Holding a special sale, she quickly made $250,000 in cash and paid off the loan. Once out of debt, Blumkin operated on a cash-only basis and provided her customers with a wide range of quality products selling for 20 percent to 30 percent below normal retail. One of the first to use the "superstore" concept successfully, Rose Blumkin sold Nebraska Furniture Mart in 1983 for $60 million in a "handshake deal."

CONSIDER THIS: When times are good, getting into debt is easy, but when times are bad, debt can be fatal.

Curt Carlson and Gold Bond

"Success is sweat plus effort."
—A. A. MILNE

THE SON OF Swedish immigrants, Curt Carlson was born into a family that stressed hard work, religious training, and the importance of family. By the time he had reached the age of eleven, Curt had his first paper route. While he was in college, he operated a corner newsstand and sold advertising. After Curt graduated with a degree in economics, he went to work as a soap salesman for Procter & Gamble. When he noticed a department store giving away redeemable coupons for each dollar's worth of merchandise purchased, Curt thought the trading stamps also could build business for grocery stores. In 1938 he started the Gold Bond Stamp Company, and spent his evenings and weekends selling the idea to mom-and-pop groceries in Minneapolis, Minnesota. The concept caught on slowly at first, but soon Curt quit his full-time job to devote time to his new venture.

Just as the business was starting to take off, World War II paralyzed the market. The company managed to survive, and by the 1950s Gold Bond stamps were being offered by national chain stores. In the 1960s the trading stamp business peaked, and Curt Carlson began to diversify. He purchased the prestigious Radisson Hotel in Minneapolis and began to build a large chain of hotels throughout the United States and Canada. Other Carlson holdings include restaurants, marketing companies, travel agencies, and investment firms. Carlson has also taken a leadership role in supporting non-profit organizations. His company is a charter member of the Minnesota Keystone Club, which consists of businesses that donate 5 percent of their earnings to selected local organizations.

CONSIDER THIS: Working hard and smart can still get you to the top. But don't leave it at that, add persistence and patience.

The Slinky

"The man with a new idea is a crank until his idea succeeds."
—MARK TWAIN

OPPORTUNITY OFTEN KNOCKS at odd times and in odd ways. When the knock occurs, some people answer the door, say "What a great idea!" and then proceed to do little or nothing about it. A few people will grab the opportunity and make something happen. The Slinky, the spring-like toy that walks down stairs, essentially invented itself. One day in 1943, Richard James, a marine engineer, was startled by a zero-compression spring that fell off a shelf, proceeded to "walk" across a row of books, and then bounced to the floor. James took the spring home, and his toddler played with it for hours. The spring represented an opportunity. What could be done with it? Along with his wife, Betty, James decided to test the potential of marketing the spring as a toy. They made 100 of the springs and arranged to show them at Gimbel's department store in New York City. Customers loved the Slinky's "personality" and bought the entire stock.

Manufacture, promotion, and distribution of the Slinky was haphazard at first, but sales soon flourished. Unfortunately, Richard had a difficult time coping with success. By the mid-1950s, he had drained the company of most of its assets. After Richard left his wife and the Slinky organization, Betty continued on her own and returned the business to prosperity. After more than fifty years, and with only small modifications, the Slinky still has the appeal to become a favorite toy of each new generation.

CONSIDER THIS: Look at simple things. Get good ideas. Get feedback. If the idea is good, then add very hard work. The formula spells success.

Harriet Tubman

*"That this nation, under God, shall have
a new birth of freedom."*
—ABRAHAM LINCOLN

WITHOUT FREEDOM, THERE would be no American Dream. The freedom that allows us to have such a dream has been secured by many great Americans who risked their own lives for the benefit of others. Harriet Tubman, a slave born in Maryland in 1820, became one of America's fighters for freedom. She had heard stories about a land in the north where black people could be free. At night, she dreamed of that land and looked into the deep night sky to find the North Star. That was the star that would lead to "the promised land." Other slaves talked about an Underground Railroad, a network of people who would help slaves find freedom.

Harriet knew she had to find that railroad before it was too late. One day she learned that she was to be sold away from her husband and sent farther south where it was much more difficult for slaves to escape. That night, Harriet made her move.

She escaped first to the house of a woman she knew was a member of the Underground Railroad. From that point, Harriet was led farther and farther north, from station to station, until she walked into Pennsylvania and freedom. Former slaves worked as conductors on the railroad and would return to the South to lead slaves out. Harriet joined the railroad and risked her life to lead over 300 slaves to freedom. She became known as Moses, after the biblical figure who cried "Let my people go." After the Civil War, Harriet tended to the poor in her house in Albany, New York, until her death in 1913.

CONSIDER THIS: Freedom is a first and necessary step in realizing our dreams.

Celestial Seasonings

"Good taste is the flower of good sense."
—A. POINCELOT

JUST FOR HIS own pleasure, Mo Siegel picked herbs in the mountains of Colorado and blended them to make an herbal tea. His friends loved the tea and encouraged him to sell the blend. Mo experimented with selling small amounts of his concoction at some local health food stores, and customers seemed to like it very much. Although his small experiment was successful, Mo found that creating a company to produce and sell large amounts of tea was not easy. However, the dream of success was fixed in his mind, and it urged him on. Mo and his wife, Peggy, crisscrossed the country, introducing their tea to skeptical store owners. Back home, there was no money to hire herb pickers, make the teabags, print the boxes, or pay the helpers. Times were very lean.

Mo believed that his company would make it. A college drop-out, Mo's business acumen and success-oriented attitude came from reading the writings and biographies of his American heroes, among them Abe Lincoln, Walt Disney, Tom Watson, and others. He also had a deep belief in God and had studied carefully the teachings of Jesus. Work, work, and more work slowly moved the business into prosperity. Mo Siegel was smart enough to realize that he could not know everything, and as his Celestial Seasonings company grew, he hired key people from Coca-Cola, Pepsi, Pepperidge Farms, General Foods, and other successful corporations. Workers were given ownership in the company, and their commitment to excellence in quality and production made Celestial Seasonings a classic success story.

CONSIDER THIS: Work, work, work. Think, think, think. Working hard and thinking smart are still two main keys to success.

The Potato Chip

> *"Common sense in an uncommon degree is
> what the world calls wisdom.*
> —SAMUEL TAYLOR COLERIDGE

IN 1853 GEORGE CRUM was chef at a resort in Saratoga Springs, New York, when he came up with a new way to fry potatoes. Everyone liked the idea, but people constantly told George to cut the potatoes thinner and thinner. Finally, he began slicing the potatoes so thinly that they were transparent, then fried them in deep oil and salted them. The potatoes were a big hit at the resort and became known as Saratoga Chips along the East Coast. Once a good idea materializes, it takes no time for enterprising imitators to try their hand at the task.

In the 1890s George Sleeper also made a contribution to the potato chip. He was a caterer in Massachusetts when he began placing potato chips in box lunches. They proved so popular that he built a business around the chips and popularized their use in packaged lunches. In 1921 Earl Wise used the potato chip to get him out of a bind. As a grocer with far too many potatoes, he decided to slice them on his cabbage cutter and make them into chips, which he sold in bags for a nickel each. His idea soon grew into a business, and Wise Potato Chips became one of the first producers of processed foods sold in grocery stores. Literally hundreds of independent chip makers sprang up throughout the United States in the twenties and thirties and after World War II. Many of those enterprises eventually were assimilated into larger food companies.

CONSIDER THIS: Good ideas do not have to be original. It may be less risky to duplicate someone else's success from another part of the country.

The Hula Hoop

"Experience is not what happens to a man; it is what a man does with what happens to him."
—ALDOUS HUXLEY

WHAM-O MANUFACTURING CO.'S original mega-hit product was a financial failure. It began when a friend brought an Australian exercise hoop to Rich Knerr and Spud Melin. The two were already marketing several sports articles and thought the hoop looked like fun. They called the item a Hula Hoop, trademarked the catchy name, and began promoting the hoop in parks, where kids would gather around for a look and then run to their local store to buy one. Wham-O gave away "seed" hoops on beaches and college campuses to get the craze going. The company's marketing plan was outstanding, and the Hula Hoop took America by storm. However, there was a problem with the success.

Although they had applied for a patent, more than forty competitors entered the market, drawing on the promotion that Wham-O had already begun (and paid for). It was too late and too expensive to force the competitors out of business. Although millions of Hula Hoops were sold, the fad was short-lived and, in the end, the company lost money on the toy. However, the advertising placed Wham-O in the public eye. The company became a household name. Also, the Hula Hoop experience prepared the firm to better protect its next popular product, the Frisbee flying disc. The Hula Hoop was brought out again several years later, and although it was not as popular as it was initially, Wham-O made money the second time around.

CONSIDER THIS: A loss may really be a success in the long run. It can give you experience and exposure, and prepare you for the next challenge.

Dell Computers

"When fortune smiles, embrace her."
—Thomas Fuller

NEW VENTURES ARE often conceived on the leading edge of technology. Such has been the case for many companies in the microcomputer industry. Even with billion-dollar companies such as IBM and AT&T leading the way, the window of opportunity often opens wide enough for even an ill-financed college student to make it big. Michael Dell began preparing for his big opportunity as a teenager selling newspaper subscriptions. After working on a phone bank with fifty other callers and making few sales, Michael thought of a more direct approach. He began getting information about newlywed couples and contacting them directly. Sales soared. Later, when his family bought a computer,

Michael took it apart in an effort to gain an understanding of the device all the way down to the chip level.

Michael believed his future was in computers, but his parents insisted that he enroll in the pre-medicine curriculum at the University of Texas in Austin. From his dormitory, he began to set up his business, placing ads in computer magazines, assembling the machines, and shipping them to customers. Michael's company, PC Limited, soon grew so large that he convinced his parents to let him run it full time. Within several years, his computer sales were over $100 million annually. Using the concepts of zero defects and just-in-time inventory, Michael's company, now Dell Computers, has kept costs down and quality high. Even though he is very sure of his business sense, Michael Dell has put together a senior management team from leading high-tech companies to ensure his firm's continued growth.

CONSIDER THIS: Watch for the window of opportunity to open. It is at that point that anyone with brains and determination can successfully compete against all the rest.

The Golden Rule Stores

"Do unto others as you would have them do unto you."
—Jesus Christ

Today, when we enter a modern department store, we may think of how it is run by a gigantic and complex international conglomerate. Yet, every business was at one time a single person's idea. The giant corporation is an extension of that original idea. James Cash Penney was born in Hamilton, Missouri, in 1875, the son of a Baptist minister. During his early years, he raised pigs and watermelons and ran a butcher shop. He refused to supply meat to hotels that sold liquor, and his butcher shop failed. Next, he tried retail dry goods and in 1902 bought a one-third share in a dry goods store in Kemmerer, Wyoming. From that store he launched a chain called the Golden Rule stores, so named because they were based on the concept of treating all people with the kindness we ourselves expect, that is, the Golden Rule as taught by Jesus. Every store had a giant Golden Rule sign hanging on a prominent wall.

Penney believed that every person was a "human dynamo, capable of accomplishing anything to which he aspires." He despised debt, drinking, and smoking, and he demanded zeal, enthusiasm, and loyalty from every employee. Penney claimed that it was the application of the Golden Rule that made his stores (now named JCPenney) a success. By the time he died in 1971, Penney's stores had annual sales of over $4 billion and were the nation's sixth-largest merchandiser.

CONSIDER THIS: Do you apply the Golden Rule to your work? Do you demand zeal and enthusiasm from yourself and your employees?

Coca-Cola

"Sometimes when I consider what tremendous consequences come from little things, I am tempted to think there are no little things."

—BRUCE BARTON

AT THE TURN of the century, Five Points was the meeting place in Atlanta, Georgia. Anything new in town was talked about there, especially at Joe Jacobs's Drug Store. Therefore, Joe's pharmacy was a natural place for Dr. John Pemberton to test his new beverage formula. Willis Venable had a leased soda fountain in the store, and Pemberton asked him to mix one ounce of his syrup with five ounces of water and ice. Venable drank the concoction, smacked his lips, and suggested a second round. But as he began putting water in the glass, he accidentally pulled the lever for soda water.

When he tasted the second mixture, his eyes lit up at the pleasing flavor and effervescence.

Pemberton explained that his concoction consisted of extracts from the coca plant and cola nuts, and that he was going to call it Coca-Cola. On May 8, 1886, Coca-Cola went on sale in Joe Jacobs's Drug Store. The first advertisement appearing in the local newspaper three weeks later described Coca-Cola as "Refreshing! Exhilarating! Invigorating!" Coca-Cola was not the first soft drink in the marketplace, but it offered a new and pleasing taste. Pemberton had a great product, but he did not possess the resources to make the beverage a success. He lost money on Coca-Cola its first two years, and just before he died, Pemberton sold his interest in the product for $1,750 to Asa Candler. It was Candler who took Coca-Cola from obscurity to success.

CONSIDER THIS: Even the best idea may take years and the right businessperson to crack the marketplace and become an industry leader.

Sherwin-Williams

"The world hates change, yet it is the only thing that has brought progress."
—CHARLES KETTERING

AT TIMES, YOU must stick to your convictions. This can be particularly difficult when your convictions run counter to long-standing tradition. Paint has been around for thousands of years, having been used by the Egyptians prior to 1000 B.C. By the nineteenth century, paint was sold as a base color, with pigments available for custom mixing. However, the average nineteenth-century American rarely used paint. Most houses were left unpainted, but if a home was painted, the owner usually had to rely on a painter to mix the desired color or be content with white. It was almost impossible to purchase two batches of paint that matched exactly.

In 1870 a paint company named Sherwin, Dunham, and Griswold had to make a decision. One of the partners, Henry Sherwin, had come up with an idea to develop ready-mixed paints, but the other owners were against it. They were sure that people wanted to mix their colors at home—to get the tint just right. Sherwin disagreed, and as a result, the company was dissolved and Sherwin found another partner, Edward Williams. Their new firm, Sherwin-Williams, embarked on a lengthy research project to perfect a way to premix paint in a consistent and convenient manner. The company's ready-mixed paint was introduced in 1880 and signaled a revolution in do-it-yourself painting. Soon, few American houses were left unpainted, proving that Henry Sherwin was right after all— homeowners didn't like the hassle of mixing their own paint.

CONSIDER THIS: Some people cannot see advancement. Some will not consider change. Those who can see advancement and are willing to seek change can lead the way to the future.

Reader's Digest

"Don't dodge difficulties; meet them, greet them, beat them. All great men have been through the wringer."

—A. A. MILNE

GOOD IDEAS MAY meet with success initially, then hit a roadblock when everything looks good. In fact, many ideas are laid to rest at that point. DeWitt Wallace's dream would have been buried long ago if not for his determination to overcome obstacles. Wallace had an idea for a small publication that would be both entertaining and informative. At the time, there were many good magazines on the market, but a reader would have to spend a small fortune to buy them all. Wallace put together a dummy magazine that used condensations of previously published articles. He named his prototype *Reader's Digest*. Unable to secure backers for the venture, Wallace and his fiancée rented an office and set up their own small publishing concern.

On their wedding day, the couple sent out mimeographed circulars seeking subscriptions. When they returned from their honeymoon two weeks later, they had received 1,500 charter subscriptions. The first issue of *Reader's Digest* was dated February 1922. Everything went well for a while as other magazines readily gave them permission to reprint articles. But as subscriptions increased, the other magazines began to see *Reader's Digest* as competition, and sources for articles dried up. In 1933 Wallace began commissioning articles to be written for other magazines, securing the rights to reprint them later. He was widely criticized, but the concept kept his publication alive. The practice was discontinued in the 1950s, but by then, *Reader's Digest* had become a continuing success.

CONSIDER THIS: Even when your dream does not become a reality the first few times you reach for it, keep trying. Persistence is often your most powerful ally.

The Microwave Oven

> *"To maintain maximum attention, it's hard to
> beat a good, big mistake."*
> —DAVID D. HEWITT

SINCE WORLD WAR II, the pace of American life has increased so dramatically that it appears we are trying to create an instant society. Consumers demand instant service. Many stores offer instant credit. There are instant potatoes, instant stock market quotes, and point-of-sale displays for instant buying decisions. A major component of our fast-paced society is the microwave oven, which essentially has provided man with the first new way to cook food since fire. Although it was bound to be discovered eventually, the microwave oven was invented "by accident" by Dr. Percy Spencer.

The apparatus that led to the development of the microwave oven was the magnetron, a device originally used in radar that was invented in England by Sir John Randall and Dr. H. A. Boot. Spencer, an engineer at Raytheon Company, was testing a magnetron after the war when he noticed that a candy bar in his pocket had melted. To find out what had taken place, Spencer exposed other foods to the magnetron's presence. Popcorn popped and an egg exploded, half-cooked from the inside out. Building on that research, Raytheon developed a commercial microwave oven, but because of the bulkiness of vacuum-tube technology, it was expensive and few were sold. Tappan introduced a much smaller home model in 1952, and the stage was set for a revolution in the way Americans cooked.

CONSIDER THIS: Many new ideas are developed "by accident," but it is those persons who possess the curiosity to follow up on unusual occurrences who often make the real discovery.

Wilma Rudolph, the Polio Victim Who Won the Gold

> *"He that is good at making excuses is*
> *seldom good at anything else."*
> —BENJAMIN FRANKLIN

HOW MANY TIMES have you used excuses to rationalize your way out of success? Zig Zieglar calls the phenomenon "Stinkin' Thinkin'" and warns us about "hardening of the attitudes." Wilma Rudolph is an example of how an undying belief in oneself can be the catalyst to overcoming problems. Polio took a toll on Wilma as a child. For six years she wore braces and could not walk, but she believed the braces would someday come off. The doctor was doubtful Wilma would ever walk correctly, but he encouraged her to exercise. Wilma didn't understand that she might be permanently handicapped. She thought that if a little exercise was good, a lot must be very good. When her parents were away, Wilma would take off the braces and try again and again to walk unaided. When she was eleven, she told her doctor, "I have something to show you." Wilma removed her braces and walked across the room. She never put them on again.

Wilma wanted to play sports. After some false starts at basketball, she finally confronted her coach, saying, "If you give me ten minutes a day, I will give you in return a world-class athlete." The coach laughed uncontrollably but agreed to give Wilma the time. When basketball season was over, Wilma turned to track. By age fourteen she was on the track team, and by sixteen she was encouraged to prepare for the Olympics. Wilma Rudolph won a bronze medal at the 1956 Olympics and three gold medals at the 1960 Games.

CONSIDER THIS: Belief in yourself and hard work can make you a world-class individual in whatever area you choose. What will you have if you give up? What can you have if you keep on trying?

The Rest of the Story

> *"A teacher affects eternity; he can never tell*
> *where his influence stops."*
> —HENRY ADAMS

PAUL HARVEY WAS born in 1918, in Tulsa, Oklahoma, and his father died when he was just three years old. Since he showed an interest in radio, Paul's high school English teacher pushed him to take a job at KVOO, a local radio station. Occasionally, Paul would be allowed to do some announcing. Sometimes he read the news from the wire, and he even filled in a few times by playing his guitar. Paul gradually moved up the ranks, from station "gofer" to spot announcer, newscaster, and manager. "I hung around the studio every minute I wasn't in school," he remembers. In 1944, Paul began two fifteen-minute news commentaries from a

Chicago-based radio station. He added a segment in 1946 called "The Rest of the Story" in which he told an anecdote that had a surprise ending. In 1976, the ABC network decided to spin off that segment into its own series.

Unlike the stereotype of many broadcasters as liberals, Paul Harvey champions the old-fashioned values of God, country, family, a strong work ethic, and rugged individualism. He speaks with a homespun style that, to many, has made him the spokesperson for middle America. No one sees him as a big city journalist—he's just a guy telling a story. Paul's efforts have earned him numerous honorary degrees and won him some of the most prestigious awards in the communications industry. With his distinctive style and instantly recognizable delivery, Paul Harvey draws listeners into his stories, tells it like it is, and then bids them to have a "Good Day!"

CONSIDER THIS: Be straightforward in your speech. Be clear in your explanations. Say "yes" or "no" more often than you say "maybe."

Milton Hershey

*"The difference between mediocrity and
greatness is extra effort."*
—George Allen

Some people see failure as a sign to give up. Those who
eventually become successful see failure as a stepping-stone and
another lesson in the business school of life. They just keep on
trying. Milton Hershey's father was an itinerant speculator,
moving from place to place and investing in every kind of business with little success. Milton, born in 1857, attended seven
schools in eight years and never made it past the fourth grade.
He first worked for a printer, was fired, and then was apprenticed to a confectioner. In 1876 Milton opened his own candy
business in Philadelphia, but he couldn't make a profit. Next, he

went to Denver and opened a candy store. It too failed. Milton made another attempt in New York City, and that business failed in 1886.

Finally, Milton Hershey returned to his hometown of Lancaster, Pennsylvania, and began making caramels. The candy came to the attention of an English importer, who placed a big order. The caramel business prospered, and Hershey built a modest factory on the site that eventually was to encompass sixty-five acres of candy manufacturing. In 1893, inspired by German chocolate makers at the World's Fair, Hershey began to produce his own chocolate. By 1900 he sold the caramel business and concentrated solely on producing chocolate. Hershey refused to advertise (a policy the company adhered to until 1970), believing that quality would sell his wares.

CONSIDER THIS: Failure can be a valuable part of learning. Some see it as a dead end, while others see it as an opportunity to learn a valuable lesson.

Mary Kay

> *"People and pride are the two foremost assets in building a successful business."*
> —MARY KAY ASH

IN MID-1963, after a successful career in direct sales, Mary Kay Ash retired—for a month. During that brief span, she decided to write a book to help women survive in the male-dominated business world. At her kitchen table, she made two lists—one contained the good things she had seen in companies; the other featured the things she thought could be improved. When she reviewed the lists, she realized that she had inadvertently created a marketing plan for a successful company. With her life savings of $5,000 and the help of her twenty-year-old son, Richard Rogers, she launched Mary Kay Cosmetics on Friday, September 13, 1963.

Mary Kay's goal was to provide women with an unlimited opportunity for personal and financial success. She used the Golden Rule as her guiding philosophy and encouraged employees and sales force members to prioritize their lives: God first, family second, career third. Because of her steadfast commitment to her goals and principles, and her tremendous determination, dedication, and hard work, Mary Kay Inc. has grown from a small direct-sales company into the largest direct seller of skin care products in the U.S. with the nation's best-selling brand of facial skin care and color cosmetics. By the late 1990s, the company had more than 475,000 independent beauty consultants in twenty-six countries. A unique combination of enthusiastic people, quality products, an innovative marketing concept, and an ambitious set of goals has turned Mary Kay Inc. into an American business success story.

CONSIDER THIS: People who are respected and well compensated will often be the best assets of a company.

Mrs. Fields Cookies

*"Success is a ladder that cannot be climbed
with your hands in your pockets."*
—AMERICAN PROVERB

DEBBI FIELDS BAKED a very good chocolate chip cookie that everyone liked. With encouragement from her friends, she borrowed $50,000 and opened a small cookie store in Palo Alto, California. It took Debbi a while to discover the secret of making her business a success. Part of that discovery was that she was not selling cookies, but heart. To this day, Debbi believes that what people really want in her store is "caring." Debbi learned that she had to go into the mall and give away samples to bring people to her store. She had to use the finest ingredients to ensure the best cookies, and she had to price the cookies so that people could buy them for less than it would cost to make them at home. Debbi's company, Mrs. Fields Cookies, wants its customers to experience a warm feeling of quality and caring in every cookie. That is why all cookies are served warm. In many cases, cookies that are not sold within two hours are given to local charities.

Anyone who enters a Mrs. Fields store is greeted by a friendly salesperson who will help him or her have a brighter day. As her company expanded, Debbi Fields chose managers not only for their ability to run the store, but also for their ability to have fun. Believing that the cookie business should be more like a Disney spectacular than just a bakery counter, she is determined to give people a little of the fantasy that makes life fun.

CONSIDER THIS: Selling is more than just ringing up a sale. It is a Broadway production: Welcoming a customer with a warm hello, convincing him to believe in and enjoy your product, and sending him away with a smile.

Bob Hope

"It has always seemed to me that hearty laughter is a good way to jog internally without having to go outdoors."

—Norman Cousins

THE AMERICAN DREAM has not come without a price. Countless thousands of young Americans have defended our freedom in wars on distant shores. They were often lonely, and many of those soldiers wondered if the people back home still remembered them. The USO remembered them, and so did Bob Hope. For more than half a century, the veteran comedian entertained American troops around the world, keeping their hopes up and their dreams alive. In commemoration of his unflagging efforts, Congress named Bob "America's Most-prized Ambassador of Good

Will." Like any good businessman, Bob knows his fortune came from the people. Throughout his career, his job—much like a salesman's—has been to communicate with the audience. He makes people feel at home and makes them want to buy his "product." During his early days in radio, one show's producers didn't think Bob needed a live audience to perform. But Bob knew that it was people who made his act work, so he ushered in a sizable group from an Edgar Bergen show and never did another live broadcast without an audience.

Fans were Bob's customers, and he loved them. "When I open the refrigerator door and the little light goes on, I do ten minutes," he once quipped. At army bases and on college campuses, Bob Hope not only entertained, he sold America. He once told a group of university students, "America's greatest natural resource has always been her people. In times of crisis, this nation always finds the leaders to guide her through."

CONSIDER THIS: In tough times, laughter can help us put our lives back into perspective and help us hold on to our dreams.

Richard Sears

"Our grand business is not to see what lies dimly at the distance, but to do what is clearly at hand."

—THOMAS CARLYLE

LIKE MANY YOUNG men in the late nineteenth century, Richard Sears believed that becoming a telegraph operator was the ticket to a prosperous career. It was, but not in the way he imagined. Richard was working as a station agent in North Redwood, Minnesota, in 1886 when a shipment of watches arrived. The timepieces were for a local jewelry store, but the store refused the shipment. Richard contacted the Chicago company that had sent the watches and offered to sell them himself. He telegraphed his fellow station agents up and down the line, and within weeks his inventory was sold out. Sensing the possibilities, he moved to Minneapolis and set up the R. W. Sears Watch Co. In 1887 Richard moved to Chicago and continued selling through station agents.

Everything was going fine until people began to return the watches for repair. Sears advertised for a watchmaker, and the ad was answered by Alvah C. Roebuck. In 1888 Sears opened his business to the public and published a catalog. Knowing that his primary target, the farmer, was a tough sell, Sears relied on three principles to bolster the reputation of his fledgling mail-order concern: (1) customers were given an absolute assurance of honesty, (2) all items sold were covered by a money-back guarantee, and (3) prices were kept low enough to justify ordering by mail. Even after Richard Sears retired in 1910, his original ideas have remained a key factor in the long-term success of Sears, Roebuck and Co.

CONSIDER THIS: Providing good service to the customer is not a new idea. It is a practice that has worked well in the past and will continue to work in the future.

DoveBar

"The test of an enjoyment is the remembrance
which it leaves behind."

—Richter

WHEN LEO STEFANOS stepped onto the ground in New York after arriving from Greece, he must have wondered if he would ever be successful in his new country. Decades later, his son Mike stood in the same place and introduced Leo's answer to America's constant craving for chocolate and ice cream, the DoveBar. Over one million of the frozen treats were sold by street vendors that first year, which would have made Leo proud. The idea for the confection arose one day when Leo saw his young son racing recklessly down the street in pursuit of an ice cream truck. Leo knew that was dangerous and decided to make his own ice cream bar in hopes of keeping Mike closer to home. Since he owned a candy shop that also sold premium ice cream, Leo went into the store's back room and cut a few blocks of his best ice cream, which he then dipped into rich chocolate.

Leo intended the treat just for his family, but the bars eventually became a popular item at the Dove Candy shop. Mike grew up, earned a CPA degree, and then joined his father in the candy shop in 1977. After Leo died, Mike began to think of ways to expand the family business and introduced DoveBars to specialty stores and country clubs in the Chicago area. In 1984 he presented the DoveBar at the Fancy Food Show in Washington, D.C., and began to receive orders from around the country. Similar products have been sold for years, but Mike has continued to make DoveBars with the same care and high-quality ingredients that Leo used, even though that has resulted in the bars selling for two dollars or more each, nearly four times the price of most competing products.

CONSIDER THIS: Many people care about quality and will pay a premium price rather than accept a so-called bargain.

The Frisbee

"Advertising is the mouthpiece of business."
—JAMES R. ADAMS

IT MAY NOT be necessary to come up with a brand-new idea to make it big. There are plenty of examples of businesspeople who have "discovered" something that may have been around for years. The trick is to recognize that an idea has potential and then to find a way to bring the potential to market. When Rich Knerr and Spud Melin started Wham-O Manufacturing Co., their main product was a slingshot (hence the name Wham-O) that they sold primarily through mail order. One day at the beach, the partners ran into Fred Morrison, who was selling discs that would fly through the air when thrown. Wham-O bought the rights to the disc but it didn't sell very well. Over the next several years, the company promoted the Hula Hoop and several other sports toys. After four years of little success with the "Pluto Platter," the principals decided to take another look at the flying disc.

Remembering a lesson from the easily copied Hula Hoop, they had the disc reengineered so that it would be easy to fly but hard to duplicate. In 1959 they renamed it the "Frisbee." The name originated from a tin pie plate imprinted with the name of the Frisbie Pie Company and used by Yale students as a flying disc as early as 1920. To target advertising for the device, Wham-O recruited youngsters to play with the toy on college campuses and playgrounds. That promotion worked, and the Frisbee soon caught on, becoming a staple on college campuses and at beach parties and picnics, and spawning such popular sports as Frisbee golf.

CONSIDER THIS: Your idea may be good, but you may have to learn the right way to promote it. It is surprising how much a name can do for success.

Walgreens

"A good appearance is at a premium everywhere."
—JEAN LA FONTAINE

Charles Walgreen worked in a Dixon, Illinois, shoe factory until he lost part of a finger in an accident. The doctor who treated Charles took a liking to him and persuaded him to become a druggist's apprentice. In 1893 Charles went to Chicago, where he worked in a drug store during the day and studied pharmacy at night. After fulfilling the requirements to become a registered pharmacist, Charles enlisted to fight in the Spanish-American War, during which time he contracted malaria. Although the disease left Charles in poor health for many years, he continued to work as a druggist and in 1902 was able to buy an interest in the pharmacy from a retiring owner for $2,000. The other owner retired in 1909, and Charles acquired the remaining interest in the store, which he renamed the C. R. Walgreen Company.

Walgreen trained managers and slowly added more stores. By 1927 the Walgreen Company had 110 stores, and when Charles died in 1939, there were 493 stores. Known as the "father of the modern drug store," Walgreen generated much of his success from innovations he made in the areas of the lunch counter, the soda fountain, and the open display of merchandise. His stores were well lighted and clean, and Walgreen paid keen attention to small details. He made products that were of better quality but less expensive than those offered by his competition. In 1934 Walgreen introduced display counters that enabled customers to pick out merchandise for themselves. Today, such things seem simple and obvious, but it took Charles Walgreen to introduce them to the world.

CONSIDER THIS: Walgreen's concept of bringing products to the customer in a clean, attractive, and cost-effective way is an idea that still has merit today.

John Deere

"If we don't improve our product, somebody else will and we will lose our trade."
—JOHN DEERE

JOHN DEERE WAS born in 1804 and apprenticed as a blacksmith in Vermont. During the 1830s, the state's economy was poor, and like many Americans, John headed west to seek his fortune. Settling in Illinois, he found that his skills were in great demand. The dense midwestern soil often clung to plows that were designed for eastern dirt, requiring that farmers stop every few feet to clean their plow blades. John studied the problem and came up with an idea to produce a self-polishing plow. Using a broken steel saw, he fashioned a plow blade that would turn a clean furrow.

John Deere knew his invention was a good one and began producing the plows before he received orders. When he had sufficient stock on hand, he went into the countryside and sold the implements from farm to farm. At first, he had to make the plows from whatever steel he could find. Then, in an ambitious move, he ordered steel from England and paid the high cost of having it shipped up the Mississippi and over forty miles of land. His business continued to grow, and Deere moved his operation to Moline, Illinois, where he opened a factory and convinced an American steel manufacturer to provide rolled steel. Deere prided himself on experimentation and innovation, and constantly tried to improve his designs. He knew that competitors would be breathing down his neck. Deere frequently stated, "I will never put my name on a plow that does not have in it the best that is in me."

CONSIDER THIS: A good idea and a persistent obsession for quality are two of the most important factors in the creation of a successful product or service.

Charles Lindbergh

"It is the surmounting of difficulties that makes heroes."
—LAJOS KOSSUTH

FEW NAMES ARE so associated with American heroics as Charles A. Lindbergh. His 3,600-mile solo flight across the Atlantic caught the imagination of people on two continents, and his accomplishment has been the model for many young American dreamers. In 1919 Raymond Orteig had offered a $25,000 prize to the first person to make such a flight. No attempt was made for eight years, but by 1927, a number of pilots wanted to accept the challenge. Lindbergh was one such pilot, and he worked with a group of St. Louis businessmen to raise $15,000 to build a plane with specially designed fuel tanks and engine.

The plane was ready on May 12, 1927, the same week two Frenchmen were lost during an attempted crossing. Weather delayed Lindbergh's departure, but as the rain finally began to abate, pilot and crew began to make final preparations. By the time Lindbergh crawled into the cockpit, he had been awake for twenty-four hours. The *Spirit of St. Louis* was so heavily loaded with fuel that getting it off the ground proved very tricky. With every rivet straining, the small plane clawed its way into the air, barely clearing utility wires at the end of the airstrip. The former mail pilot battled storms, icing wings, and long hours without sleep. Newspapers had covered his takeoff, and Americans held their breath awaiting word of Lindbergh's fate. Then, after thirty-three and a half hours, the *Spirit of St. Louis* arrived over Paris. Lindbergh circled the Eiffel Tower and landed at a nearby airfield, where he was greeted by throngs of excited Frenchmen. Newspapers the world over proclaimed "Lindbergh Does It!"

CONSIDER THIS: Many people try to be a hero, but those who actually enter that select fraternity often do so by planning, hard work, guts, and luck.

Billy Graham

"Although hotels, night clubs, and bars in the city were crowded last night, the largest gathering . . . packed Mechanics Building to hear Rev. Billy Graham."

—BOSTON SUNDAY GLOBE

BILLY GRAHAM IS known as "America's Pastor." In an age when some evangelists are mistrusted and considered charlatans, Graham has maintained his integrity. He has met, encouraged, and advised every president since Harry Truman. He has brought a message of God's love and the need for repentance to millions of people throughout the world. When the nation grieved after the Oklahoma City bombing, Billy Graham was called to lead the nation in mourning and recovery.

Power and prominence often destroy men whose original intentions were pure. Perhaps one reason Graham never succumbed to such forces stems from a 1948 meeting of Graham's team of evangelists in Modesto, California. Graham, Cliff Barrows, Bev Shea, and Grady Wilson were all concerned about the poor image of evangelists. The team prayed, discussed the problem, and came up with a list of actions they would take to avoid falling into moral problems. They would be paid by salary instead of depending on offerings. They would work through local churches and not independently. They also committed themselves to maintaining integrity in publicity and in the reporting of attendance figures for various religious services. Finally, they pledged to avoid any appearance of sexual impropriety. From that day forward, Graham never traveled with, met, or dined alone with any woman except his wife.

CONSIDER THIS: Integrity doesn't just happen. You must pledge yourself to it and call on your closest associates to hold you to its standards.

George Eastman

"It is indeed astonishing how many great men have been poor."
—John Lubbock

POVERTY IS A prison to many Americans. But to some, the fear of permanent poverty has led to Herculean efforts of inventiveness. Such was the case of George Eastman. In 1868, when George was fourteen, his father died, leaving the family penniless. Quitting school, George became a messenger boy for an insurance firm. He was a good worker and studied at night to advance in his career. At age twenty he was hired as a junior clerk at the Rochester Savings Bank. Finally able to save money, he intended to take a long-needed vacation trip to Santo Domingo. Someone mentioned that he should photograph his trip, which led George to buy a photographic outfit.

Wet plate photography was difficult and tedious, and Eastman soon read in a British magazine about how to make a dry plate. Working at the bank in the daytime, he labored at night to formulate his own photographic plates. Often Eastman would work late into the night and not go to bed. He experimented for three years and in April 1880 leased a room and began to produce dry plates for sale. Eastman quickly learned that his process had flaws; once he almost lost all of his business due to a poor batch of plates. By 1888 he had perfected a process that enabled the necessary photographic chemicals to be placed onto a roll of paper, which was then inserted into the camera. Known as the first Kodak camera, the device was preloaded and required only that the user press a button to take a picture. Eastman's revolutionary camera brought photography to the general public.

CONSIDER THIS: If you are seeking to improve your life, open your mind to new ideas. Try a new hobby. Improve on someone else's idea. Go exploring. You may find the adventure of a lifetime.

Monopoly

"Public opinion in this country is everything."
—ABRAHAM LINCOLN

IT WAS A bleak winter in 1933. The weather and the economy were both bad. Charles Darrow of Germantown, Pennsylvania, longed for the trips he had made to Atlantic City, New Jersey, but the depression left him with little money for such frivolity. Perhaps as the next best thing to being there, Darrow concocted a little diversion. He devised a game based on the streets of Atlantic City: Boardwalk, Park Place, Baltic Avenue, Marvin Gardens, and the rest. He called his new game Monopoly, and it was all about making and spending money, something everyone wanted to do during the depression. Darrow showed the game to a few friends, and they liked it enough to want copies. Darrow made a few copies by hand, and thinking that he had a good idea, showed the game to Parker Brothers. But the Parker company considered the game too complicated to ever be successful.

Not willing to stop because of a single "no," Darrow managed to raise enough money to have some sets printed and offered them to Wanamaker's Department Store in Philadelphia. Soon Monopoly was the rage of the city. People who normally went to bed by nine o'clock would find themselves still trying to buy Boardwalk at two in the morning. Something about the game was addictive. After the successful showing at Wanamaker's, Parker Brothers took a second look and acquired the rights to the game in 1935. Today, Monopoly is licensed in over eighty countries and in twenty-three languages. It is a worldwide pastime that even boasts a "world series" of Monopoly that is played each year.

CONSIDER THIS: If you have an idea you think will sell, you may have to cough up the original marketing investment yourself and prove that you have a winner before getting a major company to help you out.

The Louisville Slugger

"I'd have been a .290 hitter without a Louisville Slugger."
—TED WILLIAMS

PETE BROWNING WAS known as the "Old Gladiator" in the American Association baseball league. Although he holds the twelfth-highest career batting average in the major leagues at .341, another aspect of his career is perhaps more lasting. Pete was fighting a batting slump during the 1884 season when he broke his favorite bat. As it happened, John "Bud" Hillerich was at the ballpark that day, playing hooky from his father's woodworking shop. Bud invited the despondent ball player to go with him to the wood shop, promising to make Pete a new bat. The two found a piece of white ash, and Bud worked late into the night trying to create a perfect bat.

During the next baseball game, Browning went three-for-three with his new bat and was immediately enamored of his custom-made slugger. However, Bud's father saw no future in the bat business, preferring instead to keep on making bedposts, tenpins, and wooden bowling balls. Bud continued to make bats on the side, with ever increasing success. His early efforts were known as Falls City Sluggers, but the name was changed to Louisville Slugger in 1894. Bud continued to custom-make bats to players' exacting specifications, and they soon became legendary. To identify the bats, players' names were often carved into the handles. For bats created for general distribution, Bud came up with a unique marketing idea. In 1905, Bud signed Honus Wagner to a contract and put the popular player's signature on Louisville Sluggers, thus beginning the era of endorsement advertising.

CONSIDER THIS: Solve someone's problem by giving him a better tool to perform his job. There is always a demand for the best.

Jim Henson

> **"The only way the magic works is by hard work."**
> —Jim Henson

Jim Henson begged his family to get a television set, and in 1950, when Jim was fourteen, they bought one. Jim was fascinated with the medium's sights and sounds and wanted to be a part of the magic. He got his first opportunity in 1954, when, as a member of his high school puppet club, he heard that a local TV station, WTOP, was looking for a puppeteer. Jim applied for the job and soon began working on the *Junior Good Morning Show*, but the program was canceled after three weeks. Jim entered college and planned to develop his talents as a cartoonist, but he quickly got a job performing a five-minute puppet show for WRC-TV. He used the opportunity to create new puppet ideas and also learned how to make people laugh.

Jim melded traditional marionette and hand puppets into his own creations, called Muppets. In 1956, through his work at WRC, he was given the opportunity to garner national exposure for his Muppets by appearing on NBC's *The Tonight Show*. That led to appearances on such popular programs as *The Ed Sullivan Show* and *The Jimmy Dean Show*. In 1969 Jim Henson's Muppets became part of a new educational show on the Public Broadcasting System called *Sesame Street*. The program was a hit, but the major networks still would not give Jim his own show. Finally, in 1976, an English businessman provided the funding to produce *The Muppet Show*. The series made superstars of Kermit the Frog, Miss Piggy, et al. When asked about his secret for success, Henson replied: "Follow your enthusiasm. It's something I've always believed in. Find those parts of your life you enjoy the most. Do what you enjoy doing."

CONSIDER THIS: Your most creative energy is released when you do what you love the most.

Tiffany's

> *"[Tiffany's] calms me down right away, the quietness and the proud look of it; nothing very bad could happen to you there."*
> —TRUMAN CAPOTE IN *Breakfast at Tiffany's*

IN 1837 CHARLES Lewis Tiffany borrowed $1,000 from his father and went to New York, where he partnered with John Young and opened a small store on lower Broadway. The store carried all manner of interesting items but had little jewelry. But in 1848, with a revolution in Europe and jewelry prices falling, Tiffany decided to enter the market. During the California gold rush of the following year, the entrepreneur added precious metals to his line. Tiffany pioneered a one-price system and touted the concept in advertising: "Every article is marked in plain figures, upon which there will not be the slightest variation."

Tiffany & Company was incorporated in 1868 and continued to grow until the depression of the 1930s began to erode profits. The company was "rescued" in the mid-1950s by Walter Hoving, who owned the Bonwit fashion-apparel store adjoining Tiffany. Getting rid of leftover "white elephants" with a half-price sale, Hoving brought in the best jewelry and china designers to upgrade the store's merchandise and also brought in professionals to attractively decorate Tiffany's store windows. Unlike the previous owner, who shunned publicity, Hoving encouraged Tiffany's notoriety via ads in the *Wall Street Journal* that blasted poor taste in all its forms, from tattooing to a "loud and vulgar" Christmas tree on Park Avenue. Tiffany's was back and setting a high standard for good taste. In its first decade under Hoving, profits increased over 900 percent.

CONSIDER THIS: No public enterprise can exist in health without a healthy love for the public.

Scrabble

"Nothing is invented and brought to perfection all at once."
—THOMAS COLE

TO AMERICANS, FAMILY time is often game time. Most games are sold during holiday periods, and the two games that sell best are Monopoly and Scrabble. Both were invented during the depression, when people who otherwise would have been at work had time to devote to playing games. In 1931 Alfred Butts, an unemployed architect, developed a game consisting of 100 wooden tiles, each with a letter of the alphabet printed on one side. The object of the game was to select letters from the pool of tiles and form a word, with each word receiving a score based on the number of tiles used to form it. Alfred worked on his game for a decade, perfecting it and changing the way it was played. He added a playing board and gave each letter a point value. The board allowed players to create words in much the same way as they would fill in a crossword puzzle.

In 1948, Alfred Butts and his wife decided to market the game, which they named Scrabble. The couple set up a workshop and began to produce the playing equipment. Selchow & Righter noticed an early version of Scrabble and agreed to manufacture the boards, believing that the game was interesting but probably nothing more than a fad. But as the years passed, orders continued to increase, and in 1953 Selchow & Righter acquired complete manufacturing rights. More than fifty years after its debut, Scrabble continues to sell as many copies as it did in its "heyday."

CONSIDER THIS: Do you have some "invention" to promote? The best way to sell it to a company is to prove that it will sell. Is your company looking for the next million-dollar seller? Keep your eyes open for the small idea that could turn into a huge success.

It's a Wonderful Life

> *"Every time you hear a bell ring, it means that*
> *some angel's just got his wings."*
> —CLARENCE

THE FIRST MOVIE that Frank Capra and Jimmy Stewart made together after World War II portrayed George Bailey's struggle as he searched to define his own American Dream. *It's a Wonderful Life* opened in 1946 and lost over a half-million dollars. It lay virtually forgotten in film vaults until the video and cable revolution sparked a renewed interest in older films. When the film sprang to life again as a Christmas television film, it quickly became a beloved classic.

In the movie, George Bailey dreams of traveling the world and seeing mysterious and exotic places. Unfortunately, his plans always seem to be thwarted by circumstances. George "postpones" his travels to help his family's small savings and loan bank protect townspeople from a greedy banker. When George falls in love with Mary Hatch, they plan an elaborate honeymoon, only to have their plans shattered when there is a run on the bank. Then, when his Uncle Billy misplaces an $8,000 deposit just as bank examiners arrive, George faces certain ruin and humiliation. He wishes he'd never been born. An angel second-class, Clarence, grants his wish and lets George see what his hometown would be like if he'd never been born. George finds formerly pastoral Bedford Falls filled with mean, poor, and unhappy people. He desperately begs to return to his family, even if it means he must face the grim consequences. When Clarence grants his wish, George returns home and learns that his friends have banded together to replace the missing bank funds. He realizes that true wealth is not measured in possessions, but in faith, family, and friends.

CONSIDER THIS: Wealth and power are fleeting. Faith, Hope, and Love are the true building blocks of a lasting and wonderful life.